Eight Critical Questions for Mourners...

And The Answers That Will Help You Heal

Also by Alan Wolfelt

Healing A Child's Grieving Heart:
100 Practical Ideas for Families, Friends and Caregivers

Healing A Friend's Grieving Heart:
100 Practical Ideas for Helping
Someone You Love Through Loss

Healing A Teen's Grieving Heart:
100 Practical Ideas for Families, Friends and Caregivers

Healing Your Grieving Heart:
100 Practical Ideas

Healing Your Grieving Soul:
100 Spiritual Practices for Mourners

Living in the Shadow of the Ghosts
of Grief: Step Into the Light

The Journey Through Grief:
Reflections on Healing

Understanding Your Grief:
Ten Essential Touchstones for
Finding Hope and Healing Your Heart

The Understanding Your Grief Journal:
Exploring the Ten Essential Touchstones

Eight Critical Questions for Mourners...

And The Answers That Will Help You Heal

Alan D. Wolfelt, Ph.D.

Companion
PRESS

Fort Collins, Colorado

An imprint of the Center for Loss and Life Transition

Companion Press is an imprint of the Center for Loss and
Life Transition, 3735 Broken Bow Road, Fort Collins,
Colorado 80526, 970-266-6050, www.centerforloss.com

Printed in the United States of America

19 18 17 16 15 14 13 12 11 10   5 4 3 2 1

ISBN 978-1-879651-62-3

This book is lovingly dedicated in tender memory of
those in my life who have gone before me.

And to those who dare to mourn in courageous ways
that allow them to live well and love well.

Introduction

"The main thing in life is not to
be afraid to be human."
—Pablo Casals

To be human means coming to know loss as part of our lives. Throughout our lives, every one of us will experience unwanted endings, unexpected twists, and unhappy challenges that can leave us feeling overwhelmed. Because loss and grief are part of our human condition, we experience them daily.

Loss takes many forms. Many losses, or "little griefs," occur as we journey through life. Not all are as painful as others; they do not always disconnect us from ourselves. Yet, many losses do invite us into the wilderness, leaving us disconnected from both ourselves and the outside world.

"One of the realities of grief and loss is that the rest of the world seems to keep on going forward, while you feel like you have been stopped in your tracks."
—Alan D. Wolfelt

Yes, life involves almost all of us in losses that stop us in our tracks and demand our attention. As I sit down to pen this book, my mother is in hospice care. In addition, my wife, three children, and our three pups mourn the

The wilderness of your grief

You might think of your grief as a wilderness—a vast, inhospitable forest. You are in the wilderness now. You are in the midst of unfamiliar and often brutal surroundings. You are cold and tired. Yet you must journey through this wilderness. To find your way out, you must become acquainted with its terrain and learn to follow the sometimes hard-to-find trail that leads to healing.

recent loss of our home to a devastating fire. While I have dedicated my life to "companioning" others in grief, once again I am reminded that none of us are immune from being stopped in our tracks and facing our life losses. Nothing is permanently anything.

Everything that begins leads to an end.

Our losses forever change us and the course of our lives. This does not mean that we will not find renewal, meaning, and purpose again. However, the reality is simply that we will never be the same. We are transformed by our life losses.

Loss can be sudden and unexpected, as in an accident; gradual, as in a chronic long-term illness; or prolonged, as when a person is kept alive by advanced medical technologies. Loss can be predictable, as when our bodies age and decline, or traumatic, as when a fatal illness ravages the body of a precious child, assaulting our sense of "life order," which says that parents should precede their children in death.

Loss can be partial, uncertain, unending, or complete. Loss can result from the breakup of a love relationship, the loss of a job, a dream, a hope, or a goal. Loss can be brought about through floods, fires, earthquakes, tornadoes, or by war, homicide, burglary, or rape. There are also losses that come from the broken family: the alcoholic parent, the drug-dependent child, the devastating divorce, the geographical move that leaves behind family and friends.

Yes, even in the happiest of families, loss surrounds us and demands our attention.

Even when we attend to our life losses, they lie in wait to be reawakened. Past losses are reopened by current losses. And current losses, or memories of past losses, naturally initiate fear of potential losses in the future. Our general openness to what life brings is anchored in how we consciously mourn as our life journeys unfold.

This book, directed from my heart to your heart, is an invitation to explore eight critical questions when loss enters your life. While the questions and their answers may help you with life losses of all kinds, they are particularly focused on what is usually the most difficult type of loss: the death of someone loved.

I believe we came into the world organically equipped to want to mourn our life losses.

Unless we try to go around or numb our feelings, we can instinctively feel sad, mad, or anxious, to name but a few emotions we might experience when loss impacts our lives. The very fact that we are capable of mourning teaches us that we are meant to gently face losses and integrate them into our lives.

Our very nature, like nature itself, is intended to befriend losses, rather than to deny them. Each and every one of the givens of life represents some form or shape of loss. Each one of us has the obligation and responsibility to take our losses seriously and to "attend" to them with passion and purpose. If you were to buy into society's all-too-common denial of the need to mourn, you might lose your chance for the gentle strength and grace that difficult life conditions demand.

Grief, when denied or ignored, can result in what I call "carried grief." When you experience a loss but do not mourn the normal and necessary feelings of grief, you "carry" that grief forward into your future. This carried grief results in a muting of your spirit, your *divine spark*— "that which gives depth and purpose to your living." And, when your spirit is muted, there is an ongoing drag on your ability to live life with meaning and purpose. Actually, when you inhibit the instinctual need to mourn, you risk being among the "living dead."

Movement in your mourning is not a function of time.

In fact, grief waits on welcome, not on time.

Grace: The knowing that you are not alone, that you are always accompanied. Grace expands your will by giving you a courage you did not have before. Grace invites you to befriend your grief and mourn your life losses.

Facing your losses is how you will discover your freedom to live until you die. It is up to you to allow for the mourning that all of life's losses require. It is up to you to learn to trust that authentic mourning is how you integrate losses and rise again to what comes next. That is how healing begins!

When loss enters your life, you are faced with many choices.

I have come to believe that the questions you ask and the answers you choose will determine how your loss transforms you and whether you will go on to discover a reaffirmation of life.

The questions you ask and the choices you make can and will alter the direction of your life. This book is intended as a *roadmap* to help guide you in exploring some critical questions and choices that are before you. It is a marked trail through the wilderness of your grief. The answers to the questions will help you clarify your experiences and encourage you to make choices that honor the transformative nature of grief.

Posing discerning questions to yourself will allow you to decide among different paths. Your responses to those questions can either take you on a path to your highest self or on a path that reflects your lowest self.

Without a roadmap, I find that many people stumble through grief with the faint hope that maybe one day they will wake up and time will have healed the wound. Yet, as I previously noted, grief doesn't wait on time, it waits on welcome. Your willingness to explore the questions in this book can and will allow you to create a future filled with meaning and purpose. Out of the dark can and will come light. Asking the right questions and making choices helps offer you *hope* and invites you to have *courage*.

Hope: an expectation of a good that is yet to be

Courage: from the old French word (*coeur*) for "heart." When loss wounds your heart, the wound also creates an opening for your heart to engage, to muster the courage to authentically mourn.

Recognizing your divine spark

People in grief often come to see me at the Center for
Loss and Life Transition and start by saying something
like, "I'm not sure I want to go on living" or, "I'm not
sure I'd mind if I didn't wake up tomorrow." The losses
that have touched their lives have naturally muted
their divine sparks. A vital part of my helping role is to
patiently "companion" them in ways that allow them to
relight their divine sparks.

I believe that each and every one of us as humans has a
divine spark that is the keeper or host of our life forces.
My experiences with grief, both personally and in my role
as a caregiver to others, have taught me that the questions
we ask in our times of loss and the choices we make will
either help reignite our divine sparks, or diminish or even
put them out.

Posing questions that help relight your divine spark will
invite you to experience the gentle strength, courage,
and grace you will need to slowly, over time and with
no rewards for speed, live and love again. If you do not

nurture your divine spark back toward light and life, you run the risk of becoming chronically depressed, anxious, and cynical about life and love.

A muted divine spark is always in danger of being extinguished, whereas a reignited divine spark shines brightly, with enough power to sustain itself even when more sorrows cross your life's path.

Your divine spark is your essence. Relighting it occurs not by ignoring it but by attending to it. You are faced with the need to nurture and be nurtured right now in ways that slowly bring your divine spark back to life. The questions you ask and the choices you make will either relight your divine spark or put it out. Of course, my hope is to help you make life-enhancing choices that not only relight it but help it burn bright.

Each of us as fellow travelers in grief needs the warmth and glow of everyone else's divine sparks, as well. We need to know that each of our divine sparks is being nurtured and watched over. The questions that I invite you to explore in the pages that follow are my way of trying to nurture and watch over you. My hope is this roadmap will help guide you in making choices that help relight your divine spark.

The eight practical questions you will discover in these pages—what I have chosen to call "questions of discernment surrounding grief and loss"—will perhaps inspire you to authentically mourn in ways that breathe life into your wounded soul.

Your answers to these questions will help clarify your thinking and support you in making the choices that will relight your divine spark. Here are the questions that have helped me on my path. I humbly hope they help you on yours.

Discernment

When you are "discerning," you are using your powers of understanding—intellectual, emotional, and spiritual powers—to distinguish what is good versus bad, helpful versus unhelpful, necessary versus unnecessary. The eight questions in this book will help you discern how best to help yourself authentically mourn and move forward on a path that leads to reconciliation and transformation.

The Eight Critical Questions

1. Will I grieve this loss, or will I mourn this loss?

2. Will I befriend the feelings that flow from this loss, or will I deny, repress, or inhibit them?

3. Will I be a "passive witness" to my grief, or will I be an "active participant" in my grief?

4. Will I embrace the uniqueness of my grief experience, or will I assume I mourn like everyone else?

5. Will I identify the six needs of mourning and work on them, or will I fall victim to the cliché "time heals all wounds?"

6. Will I move toward "reconciliation" of my grief, or will I believe I must come to a complete "resolution" of my grief?

7. Will I embrace my transformation from this loss, or will I keep trying to get my old self back?

8. Will this loss add to my "divine spark," or will it take away my life force?

In gratitude

I thank you for taking time to read and reflect on the words that make up this book. It is people like you who have been my teachers and helped me discover the importance of the questions explored in these pages. I believe that grief is a birthright of life and that giving and receiving love is the essence of having meaning and purpose in our lives.

After you have read this book, please consider writing to me about your journey and allow me to learn from you as I have from many other fellow travelers who have been touched by losses that come along life's path.

Alan D. Wolfelt

DrWolfelt@centerforloss.com

Question 1

WILL I GRIEVE THIS LOSS, OR WILL I MOURN THIS LOSS?

*"We need to acknowledge that this
experience of grief and mourning is part of
the soul's life."*

—Thomas Moore

I often remind myself that there is no love without loss.
And there is no integration of loss without the experience
of mourning.

Your capacity to love requires the necessity to mourn.

To deny the significance of mourning would be to believe
that there is something wrong about loving. Yet, I truly
believe our greatest gift from God is our capacity to give
and receive love. Likewise, it is a great gift that we can
openly mourn our life losses.

You may have noticed that people tend to use the words
"grieving" and "mourning" interchangeably. There is a
critical distinction, however. We as humans move toward
integrating loss into our lives not just by grieving, but

by mourning. You will move toward "reconciliation" (see p. 42) not just by grieving, but through active and intentional mourning. So, what is the distinction?

Grief is the constellation of internal thoughts and feelings we have when someone we love dies.

Think of grief as the container. It holds your thoughts, feelings, and images of your experience when someone you love dies. In other words, grief is the internal meaning given to the experience of loss.

Mourning is when you take the grief you have on the inside and express it outside of yourself.

Another way of defining mourning is "grief gone public" or "the outward expression of grief." There is no one right or only way to mourn. Talking about the person who died, crying, expressing your thoughts and feelings through art or music, journaling, praying, and celebrating

Bereavement: originates from the word "reave," meaning "to be dispossessed" or "to be robbed." It also means "to be torn apart" and "to have special needs." When you experience the death of someone loved, you are dispossessed of something very precious to you. Bereavement initiates grief, and grief tries to instinctively convert to mourning. The experiences of grief and mourning alert compassionate people around you that you have special needs that call for support and comfort.

special anniversary dates that held meaning for the person who died are just a few examples of mourning.

Making the choice to not just grieve but authentically mourn provides you the courage and confidence to integrate the death of someone loved into your life. I have come to believe that to heal your grief, you must mourn it. To go on to ultimately "live well," you must "mourn well." By mourning well, I mean openly and honestly expressing your thoughts and feelings from the inside to the outside—no pretense, no repression, no inhibitions. Somewhere in the collision between the heart, which searches for permanency and connection, and the brain, which acknowledges separation and loss, there is a need for all of us to authentically mourn.

Authentic mourning means being consciously aware of the painful emotions of grief and feeling safe to express them. This may seem odd, because your initial response following loss is instinctive and organic. The loss has taken place, and you naturally feel core feelings such as helplessness, anxiety, fear, despair, protest, and sadness.

Herein lies the paradox—a wide range of instinctive responses occur, but you get to decide as your grief unfolds into mourning if you will truly experience these responses or instead inhibit, suppress, or deny them.

Actually, befriending such emotions is what makes it possible to experience, eventually, a sense of renewed meaning and purpose in your life. Yet the emotions you sometimes most want to avoid are the ones you most need to attend to.

Being consciously aware of your need to mourn does not mean you are "feeling sorry for yourself" or wallowing in your pain. However, authentic mourning is allowing yourself to accept and to experience the natural rhythms that accompany the journey. Authentic mourning is anchored in making the conscious choice to allow yourself to mourn, to recognize that darkness sometimes precedes light, and to seek healing, repair, and transformation of your very being.

Of course, there are a multitude of reasons you might choose to grieve and not mourn. Your pain may seem intolerable. Since mourning won't bring back your lost love, you may rationally try to "put it behind you." After all, you tell yourself, mourning won't bring the person back.

People around you often think they are helping when they say things like "carry on," "keep your chin up," and "keep busy." Or, you may feel that if you don't "overcome" the loss, you are not living up to your testimony of faith that you have tried to live by. No doubt, some people—or maybe you yourself—may suggest that sufficient time has passed and that you should be "done" or "finished" with your grief and mourning.

Perhaps as a child or teen you were taught in your family not to express grief in front of others. Or, some people have shared with me they fear they will "go crazy" if they allow themselves to encounter their grief. Or, perhaps you have decided to deny or repress your grief because you feel it interferes with your ability to function at work and/or home.

All of these potential reasons and many more are often rooted in a reluctance to feel the pain of loss and a general attitude toward grief that is present in our "mourning-avoidant" culture. There is a widespread lack of understanding about how to befriend painful grief energies and use those energies for healing and transformation.

The opposite of befriending pain and allowing ourselves to mourn is control.

Underneath the controlling impulse is fear: the fear that we will experience feelings that are painful.

As grief enters our lives, many of us have been taught that giving these feelings too much attention is a sign of weakness or breakdown. In fact, many people try to head off losses in the first place by controlling. After all, you don't have to grieve and mourn if everything comes out your way.

I believe we control because we are afraid of the emotions that grief brings our way. We don't like being overcome by the waves of grief and sorrow. We don't like "losing control." And until we come to realize there is a natural, normal mourning experience that can result in meaningful transformation, we have little awareness of the need to experience the pain we call grief.

In addition, the emotions of grief are often referred to as "negative," as if they are inherently bad feelings. This judgment feeds our culture's attitude that these emotions should be denied or overcome. Married to this observed truth is the reality that society gives us little permission to openly mourn. We realize that the better we appear to be coping, the easier it is for people to be around us. People invite you to assure them how "well" you are doing and generally encourage you to "keep busy" and "keep your chin up." Sadly, authentic mourning is often seen as a weakness, a flaw, or a self-indulgence, instead of an emotional and spiritual necessity.

So, unfortunately, there are a multitude of forces working against your organic instinct to mourn in the face of loss. The choice to experience and express your grief to its fullest can indeed be difficult in our mourning-avoidant culture. Yet, no matter how difficult, if you do make the choice to authentically mourn in the ways that are unique to your being, you will have begun to return to life, to living, and to loving! If you come to embrace the truth that mourning is a natural extension of loving, you will come to see mourning as part of the natural order of life.

So, ask yourself each day this critical question: "Will I grieve this loss, or will I mourn this loss?"

Having the courage to mourn can breathe life back into your divine spark. Choosing to authentically mourn can and will help you experience a time of release and renewal. Of course, this does not mean your journey is over and done, but it does mean you are empowering yourself. To empower means to give or add power, to propel. When you empower yourself through mourning, you will begin to feel a gentle strength that runs through your body and your soul. Yes, asking and answering this critical question can help empower you.

Declare Your Intent:

Place your hand on your heart and say out loud...
"I will not just grieve this death, I will mourn in ways that empower me to rediscover life, living, and loving."

Put your hand on your head and say out loud...
"I will survive, and I will discover a renewed divine spark."

Question 2

Will I Befriend the Feelings that Flow From This Loss, or Will I Deny, Repress, or Inhibit Them?

*"I don't have to go in search of the pain
of grief—it finds me. It's when I deny or
insulate myself from the pain of the loss
that I shut down. Ironically, it is in being
open to the pain that I move through it to
renewed living."*

—Alan D. Wolfelt

Your feelings are the way you perceive yourself. They allow you to respond to the world around you and help you know you are alive. If you shut them down—if you deny, repress, or inhibit them—you risk being among the "living dead." If you lose touch with your feelings, you have no true awareness of life.

The word "feeling" comes from the Indo-European root that means "touch." To feel is to activate your capacity to be touched and changed by experiences you encounter along life's path—in this situation, the death of someone in your life. The term "perturbation" refers to the capacity to experience change and movement.

The purpose of mourning is to allow feelings to move through you in ways that integrate them into your life.

To integrate grief into your life requires that you be touched by what you experience. When you cannot feel a feeling, you are closed in your ability to use it or be changed by it, and instead of experiencing perturbation, you become "stuck." This can result in being out of touch with your feelings and will lead you down a path to carrying the grief surrounding the death. (For more information and insight on "carried grief," see my book *Living in the Shadow of the Ghosts of Grief.*)

When you carry your grief, not only do you struggle to identify what you are feeling, you often have difficulty expressing feelings to people around you. Your capacity to experience life fully is inhibited, and you begin to shut down. In contrast, you probably know other people who are visibly touched by what happens to them and to others. They recognize they have special needs when losses impact their lives. They feel deeply and they show it. They

The unique expressions of your feelings

The specifics of how you express your feelings of loss are as unique as your fingerprints. Some people are more naturally expressive, while others have more quiet styles of mourning. It seems that the important thing is that feelings be permitted to emerge into consciousness. For you, how this happens will be unique to your personality, cultural and family background, and a multitude of other influences. Remember—there is no one right or only way to mourn. Discover ways to mourn that feel safe and comfortable to you.

are not stoic in the face of loss but respond to the instinct to organically mourn, openly and honestly.

The word "heart" literally means "well of reception." Just as you opened your heart to love, you must open your heart to feel your feelings of loss. Again, we sometimes forget that love and feelings of loss are inextricably bound together. As I like to remind myself and others, the capacity to love requires the necessity to mourn.

Mourning is the experience of loss in love. Love is the fuel that inspires grief and the need to mourn.

Rather than think of feelings of loss as a weakness or vulnerability, the reality is that our ability to mourn highlights our capacity to give and receive love.

Your heart is moved entirely by what it has perceived. In allowing yourself to befriend your feelings, you will discover the natural place of grief in your life. I truly believe that place is in your heart, right beside your capacity to love and be loved. Authentic mourning, anchored in feeling your feelings, is an opportunity to embrace your open heart, your well of reception, in ways that allow for and encourage your healing.

Perhaps the most important truth I have learned is that healing in grief is heart-based, not head-based.

Modern therapies sometimes separate the head from the heart; it's as if we should somehow be able to rationally think through our grief. I *heart*ily disagree! Carl Jung taught us years ago that every psychological struggle is ultimately a matter of spirituality. The critical questions explored in this book encourage you to think, yes, but more importantly, to *feel* with your heart and soul. The sad reality is that the power of befriending feelings as a profound way of ultimately healing is often not acknowledged in our mourning-avoidant culture, which worships scientific findings and more masculine ways of operating in the world.

As a result, I remind you it takes courage to befriend feelings of loss in contemporary North American culture.

The death of someone precious to you opens or engages your heart. Now you can choose to take your heart, which has been engaged, and gather the courage to encounter your feelings of loss.

Courage can also be defined as the ability to do what one believes is right, despite the fact that others may disagree. If you choose to befriend your feelings of grief and loss, some people may well try to shame you and directly or indirectly encourage you to deny, repress, or inhibit them. So go forth with courage.

The word "emotion" literally means "energy in motion." To be authentic with your emotions is to have them work *for* you instead of *against* you. To do that requires that you put your emotions into motion through befriending them. As you do so, you will begin to experience the rewards of being in touch with your feelings and the resulting perturbation. Then you will begin to experience the benefits of enhanced feelings of aliveness, the renewal of the capacity to have joy in your life, and the reigniting of your divine spark.

Declare Your Intent:

Place your hand on your heart and say out loud...
"I will befriend my feelings of grief in ways that allow them to move through me and integrate this death into my life."

Put your hand on your head and say out loud...
"I will survive, and I will discover a renewed divine spark."

Question 3

WILL I BE A "PASSIVE WITNESS" TO MY GRIEF, OR WILL I BE AN "ACTIVE PARTICIPANT" IN MY GRIEF?

*"The embracing of grief makes me so
aware of the preciousness of life. While
I see darkness in my grief, to heal I must
seek out light. I will discover that life
and living are sacred, beautiful gifts to be
treasured each and every moment."*

—Alan D. Wolfelt

This question of discernment has the power to shift the entire nature of your grief journey. Asking yourself, "Will I be a 'passive witness' or will I be an 'active participant?'" can lift you to a place where you have the capacity to integrate your grief and discover renewed meaning and purpose. Your awareness of this choice will provide you with a participative, action-oriented approach to healing in grief as opposed to a perception of grief as something you passively experience.

The reality is that healing in grief requires a commitment and intention if you are to become whole again.

What is healing in grief?

To heal in grief is to become whole again, to integrate your grief into your self and to learn to continue your changed life with fullness and meaning. Experiencing a new and changed "wholeness" requires that you engage in the work of mourning. It doesn't happen to you; you must stay open to that which has broken you.

Healing is a holistic concept that embraces the physical, emotional, cognitive, social, and spiritual realms. Note that healing is not the same as *curing*, which is a medical term that means "remedying" or "correcting." You cannot remedy your grief, but you can reconcile it. You cannot correct your grief, but you can heal it.

Commitment goes hand in hand with the concept of "setting your intention." Intention is defined as being conscious of what you want to experience. A close cousin to "affirmation," it is using the power of positive thought to produce a desired result. So how do you use this concept of setting your intention as you explore this critical question?

When you set your intention to heal, you make a true commitment to positively influence the course of your journey. You choose between being what I call a "passive witness" or an "active participant" in your grief. To integrate loss into your life, you must be willing to learn about the mystery of the grief journey. It can't be fixed or "resolved;" it can only be soothed and "reconciled" through actively experiencing the multitude of thoughts and feelings that unfold in the face of loss.

The concept of intention-setting presupposes that your outer reality is a direct reflection of your inner thoughts and beliefs. If you can choose to mold some of your thoughts and beliefs, then you can influence your

Reconciling your grief

An important concept to keep in mind as you journey through grief is that of *reconciliation*. You cannot "get over," "recover from," or "resolve" your grief, but you can reconcile yourself to it. That is, you can learn to incorporate it into your consciousness and proceed with meaning and purpose in your life. Question 6 has more discussion on reconciliation.

reality. Setting your intention to heal is not only a way of surviving your loss (although it is indeed that!), it is also a way of actively guiding your grief. Of course, you will still have to honor and embrace your pain during this time, because a guiding truth is that "the only way to the other side is through."

By honoring the presence of your pain, by understanding the appropriateness of your pain, you are committed to facing the pain. You are committing yourself to paying attention to your anguish in ways that allow you to breathe life into your soul again. The alternative would be to shut down, be passive, and avoid and deny your pain, which is to die while you are still alive.

Move toward your grief

Facing the pain means moving toward your grief (being an active participant), not away from it (being a passive recipient). Our mourning-avoidant society, in which you only get three days off work when someone in your life dies, often encourages premature movement away from grief instead of toward it. "Carry on." "Keep your

Setting your intention: spiritual pessimism versus spiritual optimism

In part, you can choose whether you intend to experience spiritual pessimism or spiritual optimism. For example, if you believe that God is vengeful and punishes us for our sins by causing the untimely death of someone we love, it will be next to impossible for you to make it through difficult times. Not only will you carry the pain of the loss, you will carry the guilt and blame about how sinful you are to deserve this in your life. By contrast, if you "set your intention" to be what I would call "spiritually optimistic," and believe that embracing the pain of your loss can lead to reconciliation, you can and will survive.

chin up." "Get a grip." "Get a hold of yourself." These metaphors describe the attempt to manage and control what all too often gets labeled as "negative emotions." To "manage" feelings often means to move away from them. These so-called negative emotions of grief are often seen as inappropriate, if not dangerous. The emphasis is on dismissing the dark emotions of grief instead of engaging them and learning about the special needs that underlie them.

We as a culture seem to have forgotten that "darkness is the chair upon which light sits."

As a grief counselor, I am often asked, "How long should grief last?" Of course, in many ways this is like asking, "How high is up?" This question speaks of our culture's impatience with grief and the desire to move people away from the experience of mourning. Shortly after a death that has shaken you to your very core, someone is bound to ask you, "Are you back to normal?" or "Are you over it?"

Mourners who continue to express grief outwardly are often viewed as "weak," "crazy," or "self-pitying." The message is often, "Shape up and get on with your life." This is sad. Far too many people view grief as something to move away from and overcome rather than actively engage in and experience.

These messages, unfortunately, encourage you to repress your thoughts and feelings about the death. Refusing to allow tears, suffering in silence, and being strong are often considered admirable behaviors. Many people have internalized society's message that mourning should be done quietly, quickly, and efficiently. My hope is that you will not allow this to happen to you.

Remember—society will often encourage you to prematurely move away from and be a passive witness to your grief. You must continually remind yourself that leaning toward your grief and being an active participant will allow for and encourage healing.

Sitting in your wound

When you sit in the wound of your grief, you surrender to it in recognition that the only way to the other side is through. You acknowledge that you are willing to do the work that mourning requires. Paradoxically, it is this befriending of your wound that eventually restores your life and your living. To do this requires that you do not shut the world out, but rather let the world come in.

Understanding the concept of surrender

Leaning toward your grief also relates to the concept of *surrender*. Surrender teaches you that when you stop resisting and surrender to a situation exactly as it is, things begin to change. Surrender is, in part, about accepting the reality that you are unable to stop or control unwelcome change in your life. Resistance or protest is an instinctive defense mechanism you use to push away or deny your pain, to protect you from your feelings of loss and grief.

In the end, however, resistance robs you of your capacity to heal and transcend. When you surrender, you acknowledge, "This is what I'm faced with right now in my life's journey. While I'd like it to be different, I must allow myself to face the reality of what is happening."

When you surrender, you release attachment to how you feel your life *should* be and invite yourself to be in the presence of your life exactly as it *is*.

Surrender is an act of courage that allows you to detach from the outcome. In surrender, you become more capable of seeing choices that were concealed from you. In surrender, you are invited to stop trying to control what you cannot control. The gifts of peace of mind and gentleness of heart await you. By allowing yourself to surrender to the energies of grief, you create conditions for something new to arise from within yourself—out of the dark and into the light!

Reach out for support

To be an active participant in your mourning also requires the support and understanding of those around you as you embrace the pain of your loss. You both deserve and need people who will walk beside you and provide you with "divine momentum"—affirmations that what you are doing is right and necessary for you and will lead to your eventual healing. A few shoulders to cry on and a handful of pairs of listening ears can make all the difference in the world. Sharing your feelings of loss with others won't make them disappear, but it will, over time, make them more bearable. Reaching out for help also connects you to other people and strengthens the bonds of love that make life seem worth living again.

In my own grief journeys and in the lives of the mourners I have been privileged to counsel, I have discovered that, in general, you can take all the people in your life and divide them into thirds when it comes to grief support.

One third of the people in your life will turn out to be truly empathetic helpers. They will have a desire to understand you and your unique thoughts and feelings about the death. They will demonstrate a willingness to be taught by you and recognize that you are the expert of your experience, not them. They will be willing to be involved in your pain and suffering without feeling the need to take it away from you. They will believe in your capacity to heal.

Another third of the people in your life will turn out to be neutral in response to your grief. They will neither help nor hinder you in your journey.

And the final third of the people in your life will turn out to be harmful to you in your efforts to mourn and heal. While they are usually not setting out to intentionally harm you, they will judge you, they will try to take your grief away from you, and they will pull you off the path to healing.

Seek out your friends and family members who fall into the first group. They will be your confidants and momentum-givers on your journey. When you are actively mourning, try to avoid the last group, for they will trip you up and cause you to fall.

In sum, the essential tasks of an active participant in grief are the following: set your intention, move toward your pain, understand the concept of surrender, and reach out for help.

Being an active participant in your grief is a life-enhancing choice—a choice that brings the promise of hope, grace, and peace.

Declare Your Intent:

Place your hand on your heart and say out loud...

"Being an active participant in my grief will create divine momentum for me to integrate this loss into my life."

Place your hand on your head and say out loud...

"I will survive, and I will discover a renewed divine spark."

Question 4

WILL I EMBRACE THE UNIQUENESS OF MY GRIEF EXPERIENCE, OR WILL I ASSUME I MOURN LIKE EVERYONE ELSE?

"A human being is a single being. Unique and unrepeatable."

—Eileen Caddy

The word unique means "only one." The wilderness of your grief is *your* wilderness—it is a creation of your unique self, the unique person who died, and the unique circumstances of your life. So, no two people's grief journeys are ever precisely the same.

As you grieve and mourn, you may encounter some people who have adopted a rigid set of beliefs about what you should experience in your grief journey. They may try to prescribe "stages" of mourning to you, perhaps even telling you how long it should last. The notion of stages of grief is appealing but inaccurate. Obviously, if it were true that everyone mourns by going through the same stages, then death and grief would become much less mysterious and fearsome. If only it were so simple.

In my experience, grief is more like a spiral than stages.

Spirals are unending and amorphous. You can go through the same circuit again and again, but traveling up the spiral, you pass through it at a different level, experiencing a slightly different perspective each time. They do not form discrete, static shapes, because spirals can grow and change. As you allow the spiral of your grief to unfold, remember—no one ever existed exactly like you before, and no one will ever be exactly like you again. As you mourn, the thoughts and feelings you encounter in your spiral will be totally unique to you.

This question of discernment will encourage you to explore some of the unique reasons your grief is what it is—the "whys" of your journey. My hope is that you discover an increased understanding of the uniqueness of your experience.

Why #1: Your relationship with the person who died

Your relationship with the person who died was different than that person's relationship with anyone else. For example, you may have been extremely close, or "best friends," as well as husband or wife. Perhaps you loved the person who died, but you had frequent disagreements or divisive conflicts. Or maybe you were separated by physical distance, so you weren't as close emotionally as you would have liked.

The nature of the attachment in the relationship during life will in large part determine the nature of your grief after the death.

It only makes sense that the closer you felt to the person who died, the more torn apart you will feel after the death. Ambivalent relationships can also be particularly hard to process after a death. You may feel a strong sense of "unfinished business"—things you wanted to say but never did, conflicts you wanted to resolve but didn't.

Whatever the circumstances, you are the best person to describe and work toward understanding your relationship with the person who died.

Why #2: The circumstances of the death

How, why, and when the person died can have a definite impact on your journey into grief. For example, was the death sudden or anticipated? How old was the person who died? Do you feel you might have been able to prevent the death?

A sudden, unexpected death obviously does not allow you any opportunity to prepare yourself for what was about to happen.

But are you ever "ready" for that moment at all?

After a death due to terminal illness, friends and family members often tell me that they were still, in a sense, shocked by the death. I know this was my experience when my dad died. However, I did feel fortunate that I was able to share special time with him before he died and that we had ample opportunity to tell one another how we felt.

The age of the person who died also affects your acceptance of the death. Within the order of the world, we usually anticipate that parents will die before their children do. But when a child dies, this order of the world is turned upside-down. Or your grief might be heightened when a "middle-aged" person dies in what was thought to be the "prime of his life." Basically, we often find our grief easier when we feel that the person who died had a chance to live a full life. When we believe that the life was cut too short, our innate sense of injustice colors our grief.

You may also be asking yourself if you could have done anything to prevent the death. "If only I had gotten him to the doctor sooner," you may be thinking. Or, "If only I had driven instead of her." The "if-onlys" are natural for you to explore, even if there is no logical way in which you could be held responsible for the death. What you're really feeling, at bottom, is a lack of control over what happened. And accepting that we have little control over the lives of those we love is a difficult thing indeed.

Why #3: The ritual or funeral experience

Decisions you make relating to the funeral can either help or hinder your personal grief experience. There is no single, right way to have a funeral. We do know, however, that creating a meaningful ritual for survivors can aid in the social, emotional, and spiritual healing after a death.

The funeral is a time and a place to express your feelings about the death, thus legitimizing them. The funeral also can serve as a time to honor the person who has died, bring you closer to others who can give you needed support, affirm that life goes on even in the face of death, and give you a context of meaning that is in keeping with your own religious, spiritual, or philosophical background.

If you were unable to attend the funeral of the person who died, or if the funeral was somehow minimized or distorted, you may find that this complicates your healing process.

Be assured, however, that it is never too late after a death for you to plan and implement a ritual (even a second or third ceremony) that will help meet your needs.

You might choose to have a tree planting ceremony in the spring, for example, in honor of the person who died. Or you might elect to hold a memorial service on the anniversary of the death. The power of ceremony is that it helps people heal. You deserve it, and so does the person who died.

Why #4: The people in your life

Mourning, as I have defined it in this book, requires the outside support of other human beings in order for you to heal. Without a stabilizing support system of at least one other person, the odds are that you will have difficulty in doing this work of mourning.

Healing requires an environment of empathy, caring, and gentle encouragement.

Sometimes other people may think that you have a support system when, in fact, you don't. For example, you may have family members or friends who live near you, but you discover that they have little compassion or patience for you and your grief. If so, a vital ingredient to healing is missing.

Or you also may have some friends and relatives who are supportive right after the death but who stop supporting you soon after. *Again, for healing to occur, social support must be ongoing.*

Even when you have a solid support system in place, do you find that you are willing and able to accept the support? If you are ashamed of your need to mourn, you may end up isolating yourself from the very people who would most like to walk with you in your journey through the wilderness of your grief.

Why #5: Your unique personality

What words would you use to describe yourself? What words would other people use to describe you? Are you serious? Silly? Friendly? Shy?

Whatever your unique personality, rest assured that it will be reflected in your grief.

For example, if you are quiet by nature, you may express your grief quietly. If you are outgoing, you may be more expressive with your grief.

How you have responded to other losses or crises in your life will likely also be consistent with how you respond to this death. If you tend to remain distant or run away from crises, you may do the same thing now. If, however, you have always confronted crises head-on and openly expressed your thoughts and feelings, you may now follow that pattern of behavior.

Other aspects of your personality, such as your self-esteem, values, and beliefs, also impact your response to the death. In addition, any long-term problems with depression or anxiety will probably influence your grief.

Why #6: The unique personality of the person who died

Just as your own personality is reflected in your grief journey, so, too, is the unique personality of the person who died. What was the person who died like? What role(s) did he or she play in your life? Was he the funny one? Or was she the responsible one?

Really, personality is the sum total of all the characteristics that made this person who he or she was. The way she talked, the way he smiled, the way she ate her food, the way he worked—all these and so many more little things go into creating personality.

It's no wonder there's so much to miss and that grief is so complex when all these little things are gone all at once.

Whatever you loved most about the person who died, that is what you will now likely miss the most. And paradoxically, whatever you liked least about the person who died is what may trouble you the most now. If, for example, your father was a cold, uncaring person, after his death you may find yourself struggling even more with his apparent lack of love. You may have always wished you could change this aspect of his personality, but now that he is gone, you know with finality that you can't.

Whatever your feelings are about the personality of the person who died, talk about them openly. The key is finding someone you can trust who will listen to you without judging.

Why #7: Your gender

Your gender may not only influence your grief, but also the ways in which others relate to you at this time. While this is certainly not always true, men are often encouraged and expected to "be strong" and restrained. Typically, men have more difficulty in allowing themselves to move toward painful feelings than women do.

Women sometimes have a hard time expressing feelings of anger. By contrast, men tend to be more quick to respond with explosive emotions. And because men are conditioned to be self-sufficient, they often resist accepting outside support.

We must be careful about generalizations, however. Sometimes too much is made of the differences between genders and not enough is made of the essence of the capacity to grieve and mourn. Willingness to mourn often transcends gender.

Why #8: Your cultural background

Your cultural background is an important part of how you experience and express your grief. Sometimes it's hard for modern-day North Americans to articulate what their cultural background is. "My mother is half Irish, a quarter Mexican and a quarter I don't know what," you might say. "And my father comes from a strong Italian family." So what does that make you? And how does this mixture influence your grief?

When I say culture, I mean the values, rules (spoken and unspoken), and traditions that guide you and your family. Often these values, rules, and traditions have been handed down generation after generation and are shaped by the countries or areas of the world your family originally came from. Your cultural background is also shaped by education and political beliefs (religion, too, but we'll get to that in a minute).

Basically, your culture is your way of being in the world.

Why #9: Your religious or spiritual background

Your personal belief system can have a tremendous impact on your journey into grief. You may discover that your religious or spiritual life is deepened, renewed, or changed as a result of your loss. Or you may well find yourself questioning your beliefs as part of your work of mourning.

When someone loved dies, some people may feel very close to God or a Higher Power, while others may feel more distant and hostile. You may find yourself asking questions such as, "Why has this happened to me?" or "What is the meaning of this?" You may not find, however, the answers to all of your questions about faith or spirituality.

The word "faith" means to believe in something for which there is no proof. For some people, faith means believing in and following a set of religious rules. For others, faith is a belief in God or a spirit or a force that is greater than we are.

Mistakenly, people may think that with faith, there is no need to mourn.

If you buy into this misconception, you will set yourself up to grieve internally but not mourn externally. Having faith does not mean you do not need to mourn. It does mean having the courage to allow yourself to mourn.

With the death of someone you love comes a "search for meaning" (more about this on p. 88). You will find yourself re-evaluating your life based on this loss. You will need someone who is willing to listen to you as you explore your religious or spiritual values, question your attitude toward life, and renew your resources for living. This process takes time, and it can lead to possible changes in your values, beliefs, and lifestyle.

Why #10: Other crises or stresses in your life right now

What else is going on in your life right now? Although we often think it shouldn't, the world does keep turning after the death of someone loved. You may still have to work and manage finances. Other people in your life may be sick or in need of help of some kind. You may have children or elderly parents to care for (or both!). You may have too many commitments and too little time and energy to complete them.

Whatever your specific situation, I'm sure that your grief is not the only stress in your life right now.

And the more intense and numerous the stresses in your life, the more overwhelming your grief experience may be.

Take steps to de-stress your life for the time being, if at all possible. Now is the time to concentrate on mourning and healing in grief.

Why #11: Your experiences with loss and death in the past

One way to think about yourself is that you are the sum total of all that you have experienced in your life so far. Your consciousness is in large part a creation of what you do and what happens to you. Before this death, you may have experienced other significant losses in your life. Did anyone close to you die before? What was that death and subsequent grief journey like for you? How did it affect your expectations for future deaths in your life? Have you found those expectations to be true this time?

The more "experienced" you are with death, the less shocked you may feel this time around. Often people find that the more deaths they mourn, and the older they get,

the more natural the cycle of life seems to them. This is
not to say that they aren't sad and don't need to mourn,
for they are and they do. But it is to say that they begin to
integrate death and loss more seamlessly into living.

Other non-death losses in your past may also influence
your grief journey. Divorce, job loss, financial downturns,
severed relationships—all these can affect your worldview
as well as your capacity to cope now.

Why #12: Your physical health

How you feel physically has a significant effect on your
grief. If you are tired and eating poorly, your coping skills
will be diminished. If you are sick, your bodily symptoms
may be as or more pressing than your emotional and
spiritual ones. Taking care of yourself physically is one
of the best things you can do to lay the foundation for
healthy mourning.

Additional whys

The above exploration of the influences on your unique
grief is by no means all-inclusive. What else can you

reflect on that is influencing or has influenced your unique experience? There are probably other factors, large and small, that are influencing your grief right now. Asking this question of discernment allows you to understand the meaning of this death in your life and affirm your own unique experience.

Declare Your Intent:

Place your hand over your heart and say out loud...

"I will embrace the uniqueness of my grief as I integrate this loss into my life."

Place your hand on your head and say out loud...

"I will survive, and I will discover a renewed divine spark."

Question 5

WILL I IDENTIFY SIX NEEDS OF MOURNING AND WORK ON THEM, OR WILL I FALL VICTIM TO THE CLICHÉ THAT "TIME HEALS ALL WOUNDS?"

*"Mourning is a series of spiritual
awakenings borne out of the willingness
to experience an authentic encounter with
the pain surrounding the loss."*

—Alan D. Wolfelt

This powerful question invites you to reflect on how grief waits on welcome, not on time. This question of discernment recognizes the need for you to familiarize yourself with six "yield signs" you are likely to encounter on your journey through grief—what I call the "needs of mourning." Your awareness of these needs can enhance your need to actively participate in the work of mourning instead of seeing it as something that is passively experienced.

The Six Needs of Mourning

1. Accept the reality of the death.

2. Let yourself feel the pain of the loss.

3. Remember the person who died.

4. Develop a new self-identity.

5. Search for meaning.

6. Let others help you—now and always.

While your grief journey will be intensely personal and unique, all mourners must yield to this set of basic human needs to ultimately heal. In fact, your unique grief journey will be shaped by your innate, organic compulsion to explore (and sometimes veer away from) each of these needs.

You will note that the needs of mourning are numbered 1 through 6. This is not meant to imply that your grief journey will be an orderly procession toward healing. The needs of mourning are not "stages." If you are like most mourners, you will encounter the needs of mourning in random fashion. What's more, you will likely find yourself working on more than one need at once. Again, your awareness of these needs will propel you toward an action-oriented approach to healing in grief as opposed to a perception of grief as something you passively experience.

Mourning Need 1: Accept the reality of the death

You can know something in your head but not in your heart. This is what often happens when someone you love dies. This first need of mourning involves gently confronting the reality that someone you care about will never physically come back into your life again.

Whether the death was sudden or anticipated, acknowledging the full reality of the loss may occur over weeks and months. You may expect him or her to come through the door, to call on the telephone, or even to touch you. To survive, you may try to push away the reality of the death at times.

But to know that someone you love has died is a process, not an event; embracing this painful reality is not quick, easy, or efficient.

You may move back and forth between protesting and encountering the reality of the death. You may discover yourself replaying events surrounding the death and confronting memories, both good and bad. This replay is a vital part of this need of mourning. It's as if each time you talk it out, the event is a little more real.

One moment the reality of the loss may be tolerable; another moment it may be unbearable. Be patient with this need. At times, you may feel like running away and hiding. At other times, you may hope you will awaken from what seems like a bad dream. As you express what you think and feel outside of yourself, you will be working on this important need.

Remember—this first need of mourning, like the other five that follow, may intermittently require your attention for months. Be patient and compassionate with yourself as you work on each of them.

Mourning Need 2: Let yourself feel the pain of the loss

This need of mourning requires us to embrace the pain of our loss—something we naturally don't want to do. It is easier to avoid, repress, or deny the pain of grief than it is to confront it, yet it is in confronting our pain that we learn to reconcile ourselves to it.

You will probably discover that you need to dose yourself in embracing your pain.

In other words, you cannot (nor should you try to) overload yourself with the hurt all at one time. Sometimes you may need to distract yourself from the pain of death, while at other times you will need to create a safe place to move toward it.

Feeling your pain can sometimes zap you of your energy. When your energy is low, you may be tempted to suppress your grief or even run from it. If you start running and keep running, you may never heal. Dose your pain: yes! Deny your pain: no!

Unfortunately, as I have said, our culture tends to encourage the denial of pain. We misunderstand the role of suffering. If you openly express your feelings of grief, misinformed friends may advise you to "carry on" or "keep your chin up." If, on the other hand, you remain "strong" and "in control," you may be congratulated for "doing well" with your grief. Actually, doing well with your grief means becoming well acquainted with your pain. Don't let others deny you this critical mourning need.

If you are a man, be aware that this need may be particularly difficult to meet. You may be conditioned to deny pain and encouraged to keep your feelings inside. You may expect yourself to "be strong" and "in control." Yet, despite your efforts at self-control, you may now be experiencing a variety of feelings at an intensity level you never thought possible. To slow down, turn inward, and embrace hurt may be foreign to you. I hope you have caring friends who will be understanding, patient, and tolerant with you.

As you encounter your pain, you will also need to nurture yourself physically, emotionally, and spiritually. Eat well, rest often, and exercise regularly. Find others with whom you can share your painful thoughts and feelings; friends who listen without judging are your most important helpers as you work on this mourning need. Give yourself permission to question your faith. It's OK to be angry with your God and to struggle with "meaning of life" issues at this time.

Never forget that grief is a process, not an event. Your pain will probably ebb and flow for months, even years; embracing it when it washes over you will require patience, support, and strength.

Mourning Need 3: Remember the person who died

Do you have any kind of relationship with someone when they die? Of course. You have a relationship of memory. Precious memories, dreams reflecting the significance of the relationship, and objects that link you to the person who died (such as photos, souvenirs, clothing, etc.) are examples of some of the things that give testimony to a different form of a continued relationship. This need of mourning involves allowing and encouraging yourself to pursue this relationship.

The process of beginning to embrace your memories often begins with the funeral. The ritual offers you an opportunity to remember the person who died and helps to affirm the value of the life that was lived. The memories you embrace during the time of the funeral set the tone for the changed nature of the relationship. Even later on, meaningful rituals encourage the expression of cherished memories and allow for both tears and laughter in the company of others who loved the person who died.

Embracing your memories can be a very slow and, at times, painful process that occurs in small steps. Remember—don't try to do all of your work of mourning at once. Go slowly and be patient with yourself.

But some people may try to take your memories away. Trying to be helpful, they encourage you to take down all photos of the person who died. They tell you to keep busy or even to move out of your house. You, too, may think avoiding memories would be better for you. And why not? You are living in a culture that teaches you that to move away from—instead of toward—your grief is best.

Following are a few example of things you can do to keep memories alive while embracing the reality that the person has died:

- Talking out or writing out favorite memories

- Giving yourself permission to keep some special keepsakes

- Displaying photos of the person who died

- Visiting places of special significance that stimulate memories of times shared together

- Reviewing photo albums at special times such as holidays, birthdays, and anniversaries

Perhaps one of the best ways to embrace memories is through creating a "memory book" that contains special photographs you have selected and perhaps other memorabilia such as ticket stubs, menus, etc. Organize these items, place them in an album, and write out the memories reflected in the photos. This book can then become a valued collection of memories that you can review whenever you want.

I also need to mention here the reality that memories are not always pleasant. If this applies to you, addressing this need of mourning can be even more difficult. To ignore painful or ambivalent memories is to prevent yourself from healing. You will need someone who can non-judgmentally explore any painful memories with you. If you repress or deny these memories, you risk carrying an underlying sadness or anger into your future.

In my experience, remembering the past makes hoping for the future possible.

Your future will become open to new experiences only to the extent that you embrace the past.

Mourning Need 4: Develop a new self-identity

Your personal identity, or self-perception, is the result of the ongoing process of establishing a sense of who you are. Part of your self-identity comes from the relationships you have with other people. When someone with whom you have a relationship dies, your self-identity, or the way you see yourself, naturally changes.

You may have gone from being a "wife" or "husband" to a "widow" or "widower." You may have gone from being a "parent" to a "bereaved parent." The way you define yourself and the way society defines you is changed. As one woman said, "I used to have a husband and was part of a couple. Now I'm not only single, but a single parent and a widow. . . I hate that word. It makes me sound like a lonely spider."

A death often requires you to take on new roles that had been filled by the person who died. After all, someone still has to take out the garbage, someone still has to buy the groceries, someone still has to balance the checkbook. You confront your changed identity every time you do something that used to be done by the person who died. This can be very hard work and, at times, can leave you feeling very drained of emotional, physical, and spiritual energy.

You may occasionally feel child-like as you struggle with your changing identity. You may feel a temporarily heightened dependence on others as well as feelings of helplessness, frustration, inadequacy, and fear. These feelings can be overwhelming and scary, but they are actually a natural response to this important need of mourning.

As you address this need, be certain to keep other major changes to a minimum if at all possible. Now is not the time for a major move or addition to the house. Your energy is already depleted. Don't deplete it even more by making significant changes or taking on too many tasks.

Remember—do what you need to do in order to survive, for now, as you try to re-anchor yourself. To be dependent on others as you struggle with a changed identity does not make you bad or inferior. Your self-identity has been assaulted. Be compassionate with yourself. Accept the support of others.

**Many people discover that as they work
on this need, they ultimately discover
some positive aspects of their changed
self-identities.**

You may develop a renewed confidence in yourself, for
example. You may develop a more caring, kind, and
sensitive part of yourself. You may develop an assertive
part of your identity that empowers you to go on living
even though you continue to feel a sense of loss.

Mourning Need 5: Search for meaning

When someone you love dies, you naturally question the
meaning and purpose of life. You probably will question
your philosophy of life and explore religious and spiritual
values as you work on this need. You may discover
yourself searching for meaning in your continued living
as you ask "How?" and "Why" questions. "How could
God let this happen?" "Why did this happen now, in this
way?"

The death reminds you of your lack of control. It can leave you feeling powerless.

The person who died was a part of you. This death means you mourn a loss not only outside of yourself, but inside of yourself as well. At times, overwhelming sadness and loneliness may be your constant companions. You may feel that when this person died, part of you died with him or her. And now you are faced with finding some meaning in going on with your life even though you may often feel so empty.

This death calls for you to confront your own spirituality. You may doubt your faith and have spiritual conflicts and questions racing through your head and heart. This is normal and part of your journey toward renewed living.

You might feel distant from your God or higher power, even questioning the very existence of God. You may rage at your God. Such feelings of doubt are normal. Remember—mourners often find themselves questioning their faith for months before they rediscover meaning in life. But be assured: It can be done, even when you don't have all the answers.

Early in your grief, allow yourself to openly mourn without pressuring yourself to have answers to such profound "meaning of life" questions. Move at your own pace as you recognize that allowing yourself to hurt and finding meaning are not mutually exclusive. More often your need to mourn and find meaning in your continued living will blend into each other, with the former giving way to the latter as healing occurs.

Mourning Need 6: Receive ongoing support from others

The quality and quantity of understanding support you get during your work of mourning will have a major influence on your capacity to heal. You cannot—nor should you try to—do this alone. Drawing on the experiences and encouragement of friends, fellow grievers, or professional counselors is not a weakness but a healthy human need. And because mourning is a process that takes place over time, this support must be available months and even years after the death.

Unfortunately, because our society places so much value on the ability to "carry on," "keep your chin up," and "keep busy," many bereaved people are abandoned shortly after the event of the death. "It's best not to talk about the death," "It's over and done with," and "It's time to get on with your life" are the types of messages directed at grieving people that still dominate. Obviously, these messages encourage you to deny or repress your grief rather than express it.

If you know people who consider themselves supportive yet offer you these kinds of mourning-avoidant messages, you'll need to look to others for truly helpful support. People who see your mourning as something that should be "overcome" instead of experienced will not help you heal.

To be truly helpful, the people in your support system must appreciate the impact this death has had on you. They must understand that in order to heal, you must be allowed—even encouraged—to mourn long after the death. And they must encourage you to see mourning not as an enemy to be vanquished but as a necessity to be experienced as a result of having loved.

Healing in your grief journey will depend not only on your inner resources, but also on your surrounding support system. Your sense of who you are and where you are with your healing process comes, in part, from the care and responses of people close to you.

One of the important sayings of The Compassionate Friends, an international organization of grieving parents, is "You need not walk alone." I might add, "You cannot walk alone."

You will probably discover, if you haven't already, that you can benefit from a connectedness that comes from people who also have had a death in their lives. Support groups, where people come together and share the common bond of experience, can be invaluable in helping you and your grief and supporting your need to mourn long after the event of the death.

You will learn more about support groups and how to create support systems for yourself later in this book. Right now, remind yourself that you deserve and need to have understanding people around you who allow you to feel your grief long after society deems appropriate.

This question of discernment will help you reclaim your life as you mourn this death. In working on these six needs, you are influencing the rebirth of your divine spark. I encourage you to revisit this question and explore these needs time and again in the future and review the unfolding of your capacity in meeting these needs. Remember—coming out of the dark and into the light will largely be shaped by your dosing of yourself with the six critical needs of mourning.

Declare Your Intent:

Place your hand on your heart and say out loud...

"I will actively work on the six central needs of mourning."

Place your hand on your head and say out loud...

"I will survive, and I will discover a renewed divine spark."

Question 6

WILL I WORK TOWARD "RECONCILIATION" OF MY GRIEF, OR WILL I BELIEVE I MUST COME TO A COMPLETE "RESOLUTION" OF MY GRIEF?

*"Mourning never really ends. Only as time
goes on, it erupts less frequently."*

—Anonymous

This critical question affirms the importance of
reminding yourself that you will always, for the rest
of your life, feel some grief over this death. While
the time will come when it no longer dominates your
life, it will always be there, in the background and at
times in the foreground, reminding you of the love
you had, and continue to hold in your heart, for the
person who died.

**Yes, as someone once so nicely
observed, "Death ends a life, not a
relationship."**

Our modern understanding of grief all too often uses
"recovery" or "resolution" as being a destination of your
grief journey. You may have heard—indeed you may
believe—that your grief journey's end will come when you

resolve, or recover from, your grief. Through no fault of your own, you may have been contaminated by what I call "The Resolution Wish."

Oh, if only some complete and final resolution did fit with this life-changing experience. As your experience has probably already taught you, grief comes in and out like waves from the ocean. Sometimes when you least expect it, a huge wave comes along and pulls your feet right out from under you.

Sometimes heightened periods of sadness overwhelm you with grief—even years after the death. These times can seem to come out of nowhere and can be frightening and painful. Something as simple as a sound, a smell, or a phrase can bring on what I call "griefbursts." My dad loved Frank Sinatra's music. I have griefbursts almost every time I hear Frank's voice.

The resolution wish

We wish that grief would resolve. We wish that it was linear and finite. We wish that we could wake up one day and our painful thoughts and feelings would all be "over." Grief never resolves, however. While we can learn to reconcile ourselves to it, grief is transformative and life-changing.

As your grief unfolds, you may well come to understand one of the fundamental truths of grief:

Your journey will never truly end. We as human beings do not "get over" grief.

My personal and professional experience tells me that a total return to a "prior normal" after the death of someone loved is not possible; we are forever changed by the experience of grief.

Reconciliation is a term I find more appropriate for what occurs as you work to integrate the new reality of moving forward in life without the physical presence of the person who died. With reconciliation comes a renewed sense of energy and confidence, an ability to fully acknowledge the reality of the death, and a capacity to become re-involved in the activities of living. There is also an acknowledgment that pain and grief are difficult, yet necessary, parts of life.

As the experience of reconciliation unfolds, you will recognize that life is and will continue to be different without the presence of the person who died. Changing the relationship with the person who died from one of presence to one of memory and redirecting one's energy and initiative toward the future often takes longer—and involves more hard work—than most people are aware. We, as human beings, never resolve our grief, but instead become reconciled to it.

We come to reconciliation in our grief journeys when the full reality of the death becomes a part of us.

Beyond an intellectual working through of the death, there is also an emotional and spiritual working through. What had been understood at the "head" level is now understood at the "heart" level.

Keep in mind that reconciliation doesn't just happen. You reach it through deliberate mourning, by:

- talking it out.
- writing it out.
- crying it out.

- thinking it out.

- playing it out.

- painting (or sculpting, etc.) it out.

- dancing it out.

- etcetera!

To experience reconciliation requires that you *descend*, not *transcend*. You don't get to go around or above your grief. You must go *through* it. And while you are going through it, you must express it if you are to reconcile yourself to it.

You will find that as you achieve reconciliation, the sharp, ever-present pain of grief will give rise to a renewed sense of meaning and purpose. Your feelings of loss will not completely disappear, yet they will soften, and the intense pangs of grief will become less frequent. Hope for a continued life will emerge as you are able to make commitments to the future, realizing that the person you have given love to and received love from will never be forgotten. The unfolding of this journey is not intended to create a return to an "old normal" but instead the discovery of a "new normal."

To help explore where you are in your movement toward reconciliation, the following criteria that suggest healing may be helpful. You don't have to meet each of these criteria for healing to be taking place. Again, remember that reconciliation is an ongoing process. If you are early in the work of mourning, you may not meet any of these criteria. But this list will give you a way to monitor your movement toward healing. You may want to place checkmarks beside those criteria you believe you meet.

Criteria for reconciliation

As you embrace your grief and do the work of mourning, you can and will be able to demonstrate the majority of the following:

- A recognition of the reality and finality of the death.
- A return to stable eating and sleeping patterns.
- A renewed sense of release from the person who has died. You will have thoughts about the person, but you will not be preoccupied by these thoughts.
- The capacity to enjoy experiences in life that are normally enjoyable.

- The establishment of new and healthy relationships.
- The capacity to live a full life without feelings of guilt or lack of self-respect.
- The drive to organize and plan one's life toward the future.
- The serenity to become comfortable with the way things are rather than attempting to make things as they were.
- The versatility to welcome more change in your life.
- The awareness that you have allowed yourself to fully grieve, and you have survived.
- The awareness that you do not "get over" your grief; instead, you have a new reality, meaning, and purpose in your life.
- The acquaintance of new parts of yourself that you have discovered in your grief journey.
- The adjustment to new role changes that have resulted from the loss of the relationship.
- The acknowledgment that the pain of loss is an inherent part of life resulting from the ability to give and receive love.

Reconciliation emerges much in the way grass grows.

Usually we don't check our lawns daily to see if the grass is growing, but it does grow, and soon we come to realize it's time to mow the grass again. Likewise, we don't look at ourselves each day as mourners to see how we are healing. Yet we do come to realize, over the course of months and years, that we have come a long way. We have taken some important steps toward reconciliation.

Usually there is not one great moment of "arrival" but instead subtle changes and small advancements. It's helpful to have gratitude for even very small advancements, If you are beginning to taste your food again, be thankful. If you mustered the energy to meet your friend for lunch, be grateful. If you finally got a good night's sleep, rejoice.

One of my greatest teachers, C. S. Lewis, wrote in *A Grief Observed* about his grief symptoms as they eased in his journey to reconciliation:

"There was no sudden, striking, and emotional transition. Like the warming of a room or the coming of daylight, when you first notice them they have already been going on for some time."

Of course, you will take some steps backward from time to time, but that is to be expected. Keep believing in yourself. Set your intention to reconcile your grief and have hope that you can and will come to live and love gain.

Movement toward your healing can be very draining and exhausting. As difficult as it might be, seek out people who give you hope for your healing.

Permitting yourself to have hope is central to achieving reconciliation.

Realistically, even though you have hope for your healing, you should not expect it to happen overnight. Many grieving people think that it should and, as a result, experience a loss of self-confidence and self-esteem that leaves them questioning their capacity to heal. If this is the situation for you, keep in mind that you are not alone.

You may find that a helpful procedure is to take inventory of your own timetable expectations for reconciliation. Ask yourself questions like, "Am I expecting myself to heal more quickly than is humanly possible? Have I mistakenly given myself a specific deadline for when I should be 'over' my grief?" Recognize that you may be hindering your own healing by expecting too much of yourself. Take your healing one day at a time. It will ultimately allow you to move toward and rediscover continued meaning in your life.

You can't control death or ignore your human need to mourn when it impacts your life. You do have, however, the choice to help yourself heal. Embracing the pain of your grief is probably one of the hardest jobs you will ever do. As you do this work, surround yourself with compassionate, loving people who are willing to "walk with" you.

Hope for your healing

I think about the man I was honored to companion following the tragic death of his seven-year-old son, Adam, in a car accident. He was heartbroken. His soul was darkened. He had to come to know the deepest despair. Yet, he discovered that if he were to ever live again, he would have to work through his grief. So, he adopted the mantra, "Work on!"

In his process of conscious intention-setting, he decided to believe that even the most heart-wrenching loss can be survived. Perhaps refusing to give in to despair is the greatest act of hope and faith.

Yes, you go to the wilderness, you cry out in the depths of your despair. Darkness may seem to surround you. But rising up within you is the profound awareness that the pain of the grief is a sign of having given and received love.

And where the capacity to love and be loved has been before, it can be again.

Living in the present moment of your grief while having hope for a good that is yet to come are not mutually exclusive. Actually, hoping and even anticipating can

deepen your experience of the moment and motivate you
to "work on!"

Hope and faith as trust

In the Introduction to this book, I defined hope as "an
expectation of a good that is yet to be." So, living with
hope in the midst of your grief is living with anticipation
that you can and will go on to discover a continued life
that has meaning and purpose. If you are in any way like
me, maybe sometimes you lose hope and need to fall back
on your faith.

Sometimes in my own grief journey, when hope seems
absent, I open my heart—my well of reception—and find
that it is faith that sustains me. Faith that is inspired
by the moments when I'm able to find what is good,
what is sweet, what is tender in life, despite the deep,
overwhelming wounds of my grief. It is the courage of the
human spirit that chooses to live until we die that gives
me faith. Life will continue, and it will bring me back to
hope. If you lose hope along your journey, I invite you to
join me in falling back on faith.

Reflect on this: Living with hope is living in anticipation of what can be. Sometimes when you are in the wilderness of your grief, it's easy to question your hope for the future.

But living with faith is embracing what cannot be changed by our will, and knowing that life in all of its fullness is still good.

Hope and faith in God

In the religious traditions of Christianity and Judaism, hope is much more than "an expectation of a good that is yet to be." Hope is confidence that God will be with you in your grief and, most important, that life continues after death. Hope is trust in God even when everything seems hopeless. Hope is the assurance that God has the last word, and that that word is LIFE—even as you confront the realities of the death of someone you have loved. Choose life!

A final word about reconciliation

The word "reconcile" comes from the Middle English for "to make good again." This is the essence of reconciliation in grief, actually—to make your life good again. You have the power to accomplish this. Through setting your intention to heal and intentional mourning, as well as reaching out for help from others, you can and will make your life good again. You can and will relight your divine spark. In fact, in some ways, your life might be more than good—it might be richer and more deeply-lived.

Declare Your Intent:

Place your hand on your heart and say out loud...
"I will 'reconcile' my grief into my life and realize that a total 'resolution' is not possible, nor desirable."

Place your hand on your head and say out loud...
"I will survive, and I will discover a renewed divine spark!"

Question 7

Will I Embrace My Transformation From this Loss, or Will I Keep Trying to Get My Old Self Back?

*"But today I am someone else. I am
stronger, more independent. I have more
understanding, more sympathy.
A different perspective."*

—Lynn Caine

The death of someone loved stops you in your tracks and
demands your attention. While it is not possible for any
of us to stop death and loss from being a part of our life
experience, it is possible to appreciate the transformation
of our wounds into wisdom and discover what is really
important in life. This question of discernment invites
you to acknowledge the reality that the journey through
grief is life-changing.

I imagine you have discovered that you have been transformed by your grief.

Transformation means *an entire change in form.* As one
mourner said to me as she looked back, "While I'm sorry
that the deaths of several people I love have been part
of my experience, I'm not sorry that the pain of my grief

and mourning have transformed my life and made me emotionally and spiritually richer. I've learned so much that it is too precious ever to go back again."

Many other mourners have said to me variations on, "I have grown from this experience. I am a different person." You are indeed different now. Your inner form has changed. You have likely grown in your wisdom, in your understanding, in your compassion.

Of course, we need also need to acknowledge that in this case, **growth means enforced learning from life. The growth from the death of someone loved is something you would have preferred to avoid. Though grief can transform into growth, neither you nor I would seek out the pain of loss in an effort to experience growth.**

While I have come to believe that our greatest gifts often come from our wounds, these are not wounds we masochistically go looking for. When others offer untimely comments like, "You'll grow from this," your right to be hurt, angry, or deeply sad is taken away from you. It's as if these people are saying that you should be grateful for the death! Of course you're not grateful for the death (though you may be relieved if the death followed a long period of suffering). You would rather the person still be alive and well.

But the person isn't alive and well. He or she has died. You are grieving, and, I hope, mourning, and you are without doubt finding yourself changed. Even if you wished you could remain the person you previously were, it is simply not possible. No one stays the same after the death of someone precious. Each of our situations is unique, and only we ourselves can search for the answers concerning the changed self and life that will evolve. To understand how transformation in your grief occurs, let's explore some aspects of growth.

Growth means change

We as human beings are forever changed by the death of someone in our lives. You may discover that you have developed new attitudes. You may be more patient or more sensitive to the feelings and circumstances of others, especially those suffering from loss. You may have new insights that guide the way you live your new life. You may have developed new skills. You may have learned to balance your own checkbook or cook a nice meal.

You are "new," different than you were prior to the death.

To the extent that you are different, you can say you have grown. Yes, growth means change.

Growth means a new inner balance with no end points

While you may do your work of mourning in ways that help you recapture some sense of inner balance, it is a new inner balance. The word growth reflects that you do not reach some *final* end point in your grief journey.

> "The need for change bulldozed a road down the center of my mind."
> —Maya Angelou

Not any one of us totally completes the mourning process. People who think you "get over" grief are often striving to pull it together while at the same time feeling that something is missing.

You don't return to a previous "inner balance" or "normal" but instead eventually achieve a new inner balance and a new normal. Yes, growth means a new inner balance.

Growth means exploring your assumptions about life

The death of someone in your life invites you to look at your assumptions about life.

Your loss experiences have a tendency to transform your assumptions, values, and priorities.

What you may have thought of as being important—your nice house, your new car—may not matter any longer. The job or sport or financial goal that used to drive you may now seem trivial.

You may ask yourself, "Why did I waste my time on these things?" You may go through a rethinking or a transformation of your previously held values. You may value material goods and status less. You may now more strongly value relationships.

When someone loved dies, you may also find yourself questioning your religious and spiritual values. You might ask questions like, "How did God let this happen?" or "Why did this happen to our family?" or "Why should I get my feet out of bed?"

Exploring these questions is a long and arduous part of the grief journey. But ultimately, exploring our assumptions about life can make these assumptions richer and more life-affirming. Every loss in life calls out for a new search for meaning,

"Finding meaning begins in questioning. Those who do not search, do not find."
—Anonymous

including a natural struggle with spiritual concerns, often transforming your vision of your God and your faith life. Yes, growth means exploring your assumptions about life.

Growth means utilizing your potential

The grief journey often challenges you to reconsider the importance of using your potential. In some ways, death loss seems to free the potential within. Questions such as "Who am I? What am I meant to do with my life?" often naturally arise during grief. Answering them inspires a hunt.

You may find yourself searching for your very soul.

In part, seeking purpose means living inside the question, "Am I making a living doing the work I love to do?" Beyond that, it means being able to say, "Does my life really matter?" Rather than dragging you down, your grief may ultimately lift you up. Then it

> "There's more room in a broken heart."
> —Carly Simon

becomes up to you to embrace and creatively express your newfound potential.

Until you make peace with your purpose and using your potential, you may not experience contentment in your life. Joy will come to you when you know in your heart that you are using your potential—in your work or in your free time or in your relationships with friends and family.

I believe that grief's call to use your potential is why many mourners go on to help others in grief. You don't have to discover a cure for cancer. You may volunteer to help out with a grief support group or a local hospice. You may reach out to a neighbor who is struggling or devote more time to your children or grandchildren.

Remember—we all have gifts, and part of our responsibility is to discover what those gifts are and put them to use.

Yes, growth means utilizing our potential.

Your responsibility to live

Paradoxically, it is in opening to your broken heart that you open yourself to fully living until you die. You are on this earth for just a short time. You move through new developmental and spiritual stages daily, weekly, yearly.

Sorrow is an inseparable dimension of our human experience. We suffer after a loss because we are human. And in our suffering, we are transformed. While it hurts to suffer lost love, the alternative is apathy. Apathy literally means the inability to suffer, and it results in a lifestyle that avoids human relationships to avoid suffering.

Perhaps you have noticed that some people die a long time before they stop breathing. They have no more promises to keep, no more people to love, no more places to go. It is as if the souls of these people have already died. Don't let this happen to you. Choose life!

"Life is either a daring adventure or nothing. To keep our faces toward change and behave like free spirits in the presence of fate is strength undefeatable."
—Helen Keller

Yes, you have to do your work of mourning and discover how you are changed. You have to live not only for yourself, but for the precious person in your life who has died—to work on his or her unfinished work and to realize his or her unfinished dreams. You can do this only by living.

Ask yourself: Am I doing something about the unfinished acts and dreams of the person who died? If you have in any way "set your intent" to live in pessimism and chronic sorrow, you are not *honoring* your grief, you are *dishonoring* the death.

I truly believe that those who have died before us live on through us, in our actions and our deeds.

When we honor their unfinished contributions to the living world, our dead live on. When we dedicate ourselves to helping others who come to know grief, they live on.

What if the person who died could return to see what you are doing with your life? Would he or she like how you have been transformed? Would he be proud of you? Would she believe that her life and death brought meaning and purpose to your life? Or, would he see you dying before you are dead?

What if he or she could see that you have mourned but also gone on to help others in grief and sorrow? What if he could see that he left his love forever in your heart? What if she could see that you live your life with passion in testimony to her?

No matter how deep your grief or how anguished your soul, bereavement does not free you from your responsibility to live until you die. The gift of life is so precious and fragile. Choose life!

Nourishing your transformed soul

Yes, your soul has been transformed by the death of someone loved. Your soul is not a physical entity; it is everything about you that is not physical—your values, your identity, your memories, even your sense of humor. Naturally, grief work impacts your soul! I often say that grief work is soul work.

In part, nourishing your grieving soul is a matter of surrendering to the mystery of grief. As I noted in the beginning of this book, real learning comes when we *surrender*: surrender our need to compare our grief (it's not a competition); surrender our self-critical judgments (we need to be self-compassionate); and surrender our need to completely understand (we never will). My hope is that the contents of this book have nourished your grieving soul.

There are, of course, many ways to nourish your grieving soul. Here are some that work for me. I nourish my soul...

- by attending to those things in life that give my life richness and purpose.
- by trying to fulfill my destiny, by developing my soul's potential.
- by striving to "give back" what others have given to me.

- by learning to listen to what is going on around and within me to help me decide which direction I need to go.
- by having gratitude for family and friends.
- by observing what is requesting my attention, and giving attention to it.
- by finding passion in ministering to those in grief.
- by going out into nature and having gratitude for the beauty of the universe.
- by praying that I'm living "on purpose" and using my gifts, whether by writing a book, teaching a workshop, or caring for my children.
- by setting aside time to go into "exile" and be by myself in stillness.
- by earning my living doing something I love to do.
- by going through my own struggles and griefs and realizing that it is working through these wounds that helps unite me with others.

How do *you* nourish *your* transformed soul?

What can you *do* today and each and every day henceforth to pay homage to your transformation? How do you most authentically live your transformed life? These are the questions of your present and future life. It is in honoring these questions that you appreciate your transformation and live the best life you can.

Carrying your transformation forward

Tomorrow is now. It is here. It is waiting for you. You have many choices in living the transformation that grief has brought to your life.

You can choose to visualize your heart opening each and every day. When your heart is open, you are receptive to what life brings you, both happy and sad. By "staying open," you create a gateway to your healing.

When this happens you will know that the long nights of suffering in the wilderness have given way to a journey towards the dawn. You will know that new life has come as you celebrate the first rays of a new light and new beginning. Choose life!

As you continue to experience how grief has transformed you, be open to the new directions your life is now taking.

You have learned to ask questions of discernment in your grief. Now learn to ask questions of discernment in your continued living.

Listen to the wisdom of your inner voice. Make choices that are congruent with what you have learned on your journey.

This question of discernment invites you to ask yourself, "What can I learn from this loss? How can I live with meaning and purpose in the face of this life-changing experience? How can I use this grief to bring me closer to my spiritual essence? How can I use this grief to become the best human being I can possibly be?"

When you embrace your transformation, you move toward greater clarity, understanding, and purpose, and you discover the future you desire.

Declare Your Intent:

Place your hand on your heart and say our loud...

"I will embrace my transformation from this loss, remember my past, and celebrate my future."

Put your hand on your head and say out loud...

"I will survive, and I will discover a renewed divine spark."

Question 8

Will This Loss Add to My "Divine Spark," or Will it Take Away My Life Force?

*"If we search outside ourselves for the
meaning of life, we tend never to find it.
But if we center ourselves and look for
meaning in life, it's always waiting for us,
right here in the present moment."*

—Bo Lozoff

Your divine spark—that which gives meaning and purpose
to your life—is the essence of your survival and renewal
after loss impacts your life. Your life force is that energy
that is the keeper of your mind, your body, and your
soul. Asking this question of discernment encourages
you to explore whether the actions you are taking and
the choices you are making will help reignite your divine
spark, or diminish or even extinguish it.

You have actions and choices to make, and as you go
through this process you are either relighting your divine
spark or putting it out. Obviously this question is offered
up to you in hopes of inspiring the relighting of your
divine spark and inviting you to experience the gentle
strength, courage, and grace to live and love again.

Prior to losses entering your life, you may have been at risk for taking your divine spark for granted. With loss and grief comes a sense of being out of harmony with the world around you. You begin to learn more about who you are under these conditions of suffering and pain. You begin to recognize how precious your divine spark is and the importance of caring for it. When you awaken to the preciousness of the gift of life, you discover and respect the fact that your divine spark needs self-care and lots of nourishment.

Perhaps your most important self-care and nourishment need right now is to be compassionate with yourself.

In fact, the work "compassion" means "with passion." Caring for and about yourself with passion is self-compassion. I have discovered that many of us are hard on ourselves when we are in mourning. We judge ourselves, and we shame ourselves, and we take care of ourselves last. But good self-care is essential to the eventual renewal of your divine spark.

Practicing good self-care doesn't mean you are feeling sorry for yourself, being selfish, or being self-indulgent; rather it means you are creating conditions that allow you to integrate the death of someone loved into your heart and soul. I believe that in nurturing ourselves, in allowing ourselves the time and loving attention we need to journey safely and deeply through grief, we find meaning in our continued living. We have all heard the words, "Blessed are those who mourn, for they shall be comforted." To this I might add, "Blessed are those who learn self-compassion during times of death and grief, for they shall go on to discover a renewed divine spark."

Remember—self-care fortifies you for the journey, a journey that leaves you profoundly affected and deeply changed. Yes, loss invites the big questions: "Who am I?" "Why am I meant to be here?" "Who and what is really important to me?" "Where am I going with my life?"

As the poet Rainer Maria Rilke reminded all of us: "Live the questions now!"

What are the critical questions of discernment that loss has invited into your heart?

These big questions can leave you feeling totally drained. Time, which prior to the loss was for the most part a predictable progression of events, now separates you from what has been lost. In other words, grief awakens you to a new sense of time. You may struggle with and revisit the times before and after the death.

As time distorts and the loss cuts you off from your "normal" ways of being in the world, it is important to remember that above all, self-nurturing is about self-acceptance. When you recognize that self-care begins with yourself, you no longer think of those around you as being totally responsible for your well-being. At the same time, you come to appreciate the importance of being connected to others. When you allow yourself to accept outside support and compassion from family, friends, and even strangers, you feel more in harmony with your environment. Your capacity to receive this loving support helps restore your sense of belonging.

Reflections on choice

*"There is a time when we must
firmly choose the course we follow,
or the relentless drift of events
will make the decision."*
—Hubert V. Prochnow

*"Choice, not change, determines
human destiny."*
—Unknown

*"Decisions and perseverance are
the noblest qualities of man."*
—Goethe

*"The doors we open and close each
day decide the lives we live."*
—Flora Whitmore

Lessons learned, questions asked, choices made

I am not among those who believe the tragedy of loss comes upon us only to teach us. However, I do believe that when we experience loss, we encounter challenges that invite us to grow. We do not seek the pain of grief, or strive to hold onto it once it unfolds in our lives. However, everything we experience in life becomes an object of meditation, reflection, and potential growth.

Loss and grief teach you the lesson to STOP, to explore the questions that demand your attention, and to make choices that embrace the meaning and purpose of your life and the lives of your family, friends, and society.

The recent fire that damaged our family's home reminds me of how we can become complacent about even our surroundings. Our gratitude and appreciation of our true values of daily living can get lost in the demands of getting through the day. Sometimes we tend to take things for granted and think losses occur to other people. Those true values of family, friends, and having a roof over our heads, which sometimes get pushed to the background, are truly what offer us the meaning, richness, texture, and purpose that our souls deeply long for. When we are awakened in ways that recapture those real values, we are reminded of the preciousness of life and the importance of each passing moment.

So, as you work to ask the questions that reignite your divine spark, allow me the privilege of exploring some of the life lessons grief teaches each and every one of us.

The preciousness of each moment

Loss and grief teach you the importance of living in the present moment. The here and now is the resting place for your heart and soul. You can consciously go to this place whenever you choose to. Here you can rest from the griefs of the past and the fears of the future.

In the present moment comes the richness of the life that you search for. The felt experience of happiness and joy can be discovered in the present moment. To focus all of your attention in the present moment is to surrender yourself completely to whatever and whoever is with you.

If you stay still, you may even experience the presence of God.

There are a variety of ways to develop the capacity to be present in the very moment.

Deep breathing and meditation will not only calm your physical heart but will also help to direct your attention to your innermost feelings.

Paying attention to what form of creativity naturally engages your full attention can also help you fully engage in the moment. In joyous creativity, you can enter a timeless dimension and invite tranquility into your life. Examples might include journaling, expressive arts, making memory books. Doing something creative that you love will release worry and literally invite you to "take a breather" from other demands in your life.

Feel the courage within you that grows as you embrace each moment and all that it holds.

Discernment: Ask yourself the question and make the choice: *Will I appreciate the preciousness of each moment?*

The preciousness of time

Loss and grief teach you the preciousness of time. When I hear people say, "I'm just killing time," it makes me sad that they don't seem to realize what they have. Many people also say, "I just don't have time."

Actually, we all have the same amount of time; it is just a question of what we do with it.

Profound insights are encapsulated in the seconds and minutes that make up each day of your life. You need to make time to suspend and go into neutral to explore questions of life and love, death and grief.

Loss and grief teach us there is so much to know about ourselves and the world around us. However, to discover this wisdom demands that you slow down and appreciate each moment of your life. Slowing down opens you to experience the wonders that surround you.

Discernment: Ask yourself the question and make the choice: *Will I appreciate the preciousness of time?*

The preciousness of simplicity

Loss and grief teach you the preciousness of simplicity. Allowing yourself to live simply creates more time for sharing with those to whom we give and receive love. All too often, your life can get so filled with busyness and the need to care for possessions that the simple pleasures that give life meaning are ignored.

Simplicity is less about the number of material items you own than it is about staying connected to the true pleasures that bring meaning to your life. Learning to live simply opens up more time to relax and just be.

**Life is truly lived in the small places,
the in-between places that connect you
to your soul.**

Discernment: Ask yourself the question and make the
choice: *Will I appreciate the preciousness of simplicity?*

The preciousness of patience

Loss and grief teach you the preciousness of patience. You
must be patient with yourself as your grief journey unfolds
in its own way and time. Genuine patience invites you to
experience a gentle willingness to let life unfold at its own
pace.

**If you live your life from a hurried
place, you run the risk of missing
the best parts of the journey—the
uneventful yet deeply meaningful
moments you can experience alone or
with those you love.**

I once heard someone observe, "Patience is an opportunity to love deeply, and to wring the last drop of juice out of life." Yes, patience can open up an entirely new way of seeing the world outside of yourself—a world of peace, joy, love, and hope. Reflect on how patience is a direct cousin of peace and allow it to unfold, day by day, and be gentle with yourself in the learning.

Discernment: Ask yourself the question and make the choice: *Will I appreciate the preciousness of patience?*

The preciousness of humility

Loss and grief teach you the importance of humility. When your heart is broken, it is an invitation to humble yourself. Humility shields you from being prideful and keeps you focused on the importance of helping other human beings.

As Benjamin Franklin once observed, "A man wrapped up in himself makes a very small bundle." Part of being humble is getting yourself out of the way and focusing on the needs of others. As soon as you focus outwardly, you

Humility: absence of pride, cheerful submission to others. The state or quality of being humble in mind and spirit. A sincere commitment to serve others, to separate oneself from pretense and pride.

come to the realization that your needs are not the only ones that count and you become so much more capable of meeting the needs of others. Someone very wise once noted, "The proud man counts his newspaper clippings, the humble man his blessings."

Discernment: Ask yourself the question and make a choice: *Will I appreciate the preciousness of humility?*

The preciousness of love and connection

Loss and grief teach you the preciousness of love and connection. Love is the substance and essence of life. In opening to your brokenness after the loss of love, you have the opportunity to open yourself to the rebirth of living and loving until you die. We all need love in our lives. We seek love after mourning life losses because we come to realize love is the only thing we can't live without. Love nurtures both the person being loved and the person who is loving. Love multiplies and expands.

There is no experience in life that can match the joy of giving and receiving love.

Grief and loss teach you to cherish your relationships—to never take them for granted. Grief teaches us we need others and to keep reaching out, to not exclude ourselves from the wonders of love and companionship. As you come out on the other side of grief and discover new life, you may find that some strangers become like family. Knowing that you belong helps you feel more safe and secure, more a part of the world that surrounds you. The pain of grief softens your heart and helps you feel more empathy for others who experience loss. Yes, grief teaches you the importance of keeping your love connections close to your heart in ways that sustain you.

Discernment: Ask yourself the question and make the choice: *Will I appreciate the preciousness of love and connection?*

The preciousness of spontaneity and laughter

Loss and grief teach you the preciousness of spontaneity and laughter. You become more aware of the need to look for opportunities to relax and play. When life is always predictable, it can become stagnant and stale. Grief teaches you to be alert to the surprises and gifts in your day.

What are you grateful for that is within your view right now? Look around and be in awe; consider it a spontaneous gift.

Humor is one of the most healing gifts of humanity. Laughter restores hope and assists you in surviving the pain of grief. Don't fall into the trap of thinking that laughing and having fun are somehow a betrayal of the person who died. Laughing doesn't mean you don't miss the person who died. Often, remembering the person who died and smiling and laughing is an honest reflection of aspects of what she or he brought to the dance of your life together. And I ask you, what could be better than that?

Gratitude: thankfulness; appreciation; the abundant blessing of being thankful

Sometimes it helps to think about what the person who died would want for you. Wouldn't she or he want you to laugh and continue to find joy in life, even in the midst of your sorrow? Remember the fun times you shared with the person who died. Remember his sense of humor. Remember his grin and the sound of his laughter. I've heard it said that laughter is a form of internal jogging. Not only is it enjoyable, it is good for you. Studies show that smiling, laughing, and feeling good enhance your immune system and make you healthier. Close your eyes right now and remember the smile and laughter of the person who died.

Discernment: Ask yourself the question and make the choice: *Will I appreciate the preciousness of spontaneity and laughter?*

The preciousness of gratitude and grace

Loss and grief teach you the preciousness of gratitude and grace. Gratitude and grace prepare you for the many blessings that can and will unfold in your life. Look for the gratitude and grace that surround you.

When you are faced with loss, it can be difficult to feel a sense of gratitude and grace in your life. Yet, as you reflect, you may discover many blessings have already companioned you since your grief journey began. Somehow, with gratitude and grace, you have survived. Looking back, you may recognize the many supportive gestures, big and small, you were offered along the way.

When you fill your life with gratitude and grace, you invoke a self-fulfilling prophecy.

What you expect to happen, *can* happen.

For example, if you don't expect anyone to support you in your grief, they often don't. By contrast, if you anticipate support and nurturance, you will indeed find it.

Think of all you have to be thankful for. This is not to deny your overwhelming loss and the need to mourn. However, you are being self-compassionate when you consider the things that make your life worth living, too.

Reflect on your possibilities for love and joy each day. Honor the possibilities and have gratitude for them. Be grateful for your physical health and your beautiful spirit. Be grateful for your family and friends and the concern of strangers. Above all, be grateful for this moment.

Gratitude and grace prepare the way to inner peace and the rediscovering of joy in your life. You can now be guided by something you would not find through your intellect or logic. Now you can awaken each morning prepared to experience the blessings of each day.

Allow me to explore some additional signs that you have opened your heart to gratitude and grace:

- You feel a sense of belonging in the world around you, as if the universe were embracing you.
- You experience a full range of emotions—from sadness, to protest and anxiety, to love and passion.
- You experience time when you are in contact with your inner source of wisdom, love, and healing.
- You notice a persistent sense that someone or something genuinely wants you to evolve and fulfill

your potential. This comforting presence is supporting you without judgment or conditions.

- You feel mysteriously supported and loved at times when you need it, keeping you open to the divine.

- You persevere even in the face of adversity. You create goals for yourself and set about accomplishing them with continued, patient effort.

- You experience a loving presence in the universe that surrounds you. You can experience the feeling of being personally loved by the people in your life and you can express love to them.

- You experience a gentleness of spirit and kindness of heart. Gentleness eases the way and adds grace to your life. It softens your sorrows and cushions the burdens. Kindness becomes a natural virtue you express in the world. Your kindness soothes, calms, and renews you as well as the other souls your life touches. Kindness adds hope-filled texture to every aspect of your life.

- You experience the beauty around you. You come to realize that this moment, this day, this relationship, and this life are all unique, exquisite, and unrepeatable. There will be no moment exactly like this one. There will be no other day that unfolds precisely like the events and experiences of this day. You can now embrace every moment. You have gratitude that your entire life can be found in the timelessness of the moment you are in—right now.

- You experience gratitude for being more alive than you were in the past. You are aware your emotional and spiritual healing has transformed you and resulted in new energy in your body, nourishment in your mind, and illumination in your soul.

- You experience the unleashing of your inner power and divine spark. You radiate positive energy and engage in life in ways that connect you to the greater world of humanity. You feel alive, vibrant, and vital. Now you can engage fully in life. You are not just existing, you are living abundantly.

Discernment: Ask yourself the question and make the choice: *Will I appreciate the preciousness of gratitude and grace?*

Declare Your Intent:

Place your hand on your heart and say out loud...

"This loss will add to my divine spark."

Place your hand on your head and say out loud...

"I will survive, and I will discover a renewed divine spark."

My *prayer* for you

May you continue to discover the freedom to live life with
a renewed divine spark, to have meaning and purpose in
your life each day. May you ask the questions and make the
choices that help you love fully until you die.

No, you did not ask for this loss. But it has come to you, and
you have learned the importance of moving toward it, not
away from it. If you give up, your soul dies. May you never
give up, and may you choose life!

May you turn your face to the radiance of joy. May you live in
the continued awareness that you are being cradled in love by
a caring presence that never deserts you.

May you keep your heart open wide and receptive to what life
brings you, both happy and sad. And, in doing so, may you
create a pathway to living your life fully and on purpose until
you die.

Blessings to you as you continue to explore your lessons
learned, questions asked, and choices made. May your divine
spark shine bright as you share your gifts with the universe.

I sincerely hope we meet one day!

The *Eight* Questions:
Exploring your thoughts and feelings

Because journaling is one way of doing the necessary work of expressing your grief outside of yourself—what I've called mourning, it can be an effective path to exploring and embracing your innermost thoughts and feelings.

I invite you to write down your answers to the Eight Questions in this brief journaling section. If you need more room to write, record your answers in a blank notebook instead.

Question 1:

Will I grieve this loss, or will I mourn this loss?

Have you been grieving but not mourning? If so, how do you feel about the necessity to mourn?

Has anyone around you encouraged you—directly or indirectly—to keep your grief to yourself? How? How do you feel about this?

What can you do this week to turn your grief into mourning?

Question 2:
Will I befriend the feelings that flow from this loss, or will I deny, repress, or inhibit them?

Have you been inhibiting, suppressing, or denying your instinctive need to mourn? How?

Do you ever find yourself trying to think "rationally" about your grief in an effort to control it? Explain.

Describe the feelings you've been having most recently in your grief journey. What can you do to befriend these feelings?

Question 3:

Will I be a "passive witness" to my grief, or will I be an "active participant" in my grief?

Have you set your intention to heal? Write down your intention(s) for your grief journey.

How are you honoring your pain?

Are you surrendering to the unique, natural, and necessary course of your grief? How or how not?

Identify the third of the people in your life who are truly empathetic helpers:

Question 4:
Will I embrace the uniqueness of my grief experience, or will I assume I mourn like everyone else?

I invite you to review this chapter and make notes about the unique "Whys" that are making your grief journey what it is.

Question 5:

Will I identify the six needs of mourning and work on them, or will I fall victim to the cliché that "time heals all wounds?"

Please review the six needs of mourning explored in this chapter and write about where you see yourself right now relative to these needs.

Question 6:

Will I work toward "reconciliation" of my grief, or will I believe I must come to a complete "resolution" of my grief?

How do you feel about the reality that your grief journey will never truly end?

Are you seeing any of the Criteria for Reconciliation on pages 102-103 in yourself? Please describe.

Do you have hope for your healing? How would you describe your hopefulness?

Question 7:
Will I embrace my transformation from this loss, or will I keep trying to get my old self back?

In what ways have you been transformed by your grief?

Recognizing that any growth you may have experienced is not growth you would choose, how have you grown emotionally, cognitively, and spiritually since the death?

How are you honoring the life of the person who died?

Question 8:
Will this loss add to my "divine spark," or will it take away my life force?

How are you being compassionate with yourself these days? How are you being uncompassionate?

Are there any "meaning of life" questions you found yourself asking since the death? What are they?

What have you found to be truly precious to you since the death?

Also by Alan D. Wolfelt

Understanding Your Grief
Ten Essential Touchstones for Finding Hope and Healing Your Heart

One of North America's leading grief educators, Dr. Alan Wolfelt has written many books about healing in grief. This book is his most comprehensive, covering the essential lessons that mourners have taught him in his three decades of working with the bereaved.

In compassionate, down-to-earth language, *Understanding Your Grief* describes ten touchstones—or trail markers—that are essential physical, emotional, cognitive, social, and spiritual signs for mourners to look for on their journey through grief.

The Ten Essential Touchstones:

1. Open to the presence of your loss.
2. Dispel misconceptions about grief.
3. Embrace the uniqueness of your grief.
4. Explore what you might experience.
5. Recognize you are not crazy.
6. Understand the six needs of mourning.
7. Nurture yourself.
8. Reach out for help.
9. Seek reconciliation, not resolution.
10. Appreciate your transformation.

For those of you who were fans of the old *Understanding Grief* (which is no longer available), rest assured that the same content and more is covered in this wonderful new text. The companion journal now provides space for writing and reflection.

ISBN 978-1-879651-35-7 • 176 pages • softcover • $14.95

Also by Alan D. Wolfelt

The Journey Through Grief

Reflections On Healing
Second Edition

This popular hardcover book makes a wonderful gift for those who grieve, helping them gently engage in the work of mourning. Comforting and nurturing, *The Journey Through Grief* doses mourners with the six needs of mourning, helping them soothe themselves at the same time it helps them heal.

Back by popular demand, we are now offering *The Journey Through Grief* again in hardcover. The hardcover version of this beautiful book makes a wonderful, healing gift for the newly bereaved.

This revised, second edition of *The Journey Through Grief* takes Dr. Wolfelt's popular book of reflections and adds space for guided journaling, asking readers thoughtful questions about their unique mourning needs and providing room to write responses.

The Journey Through Grief is organized around the six needs that all mourners must yield to—indeed embrace—if they are to go on to find continued meaning in life and living. Following a short explanation of each mourning need is a series of brief, spiritual passages that, when read slowly and reflectively, help mourners work through their unique thoughts and feelings. *The Journey Through Grief* is being used by many faith communities as part of their grief support programs.

ISBN 978-1-879651-11-1 • hardcover • 176 pages • $21.95

Also by Alan D. Wolfelt

Living in the Shadow of the Ghosts of Grief
Step into the Light
Reconcile old losses and open the door to infinite joy and love

"*Accumulated, unreconciled loss affects every aspect of our lives. Living in the Shadow is a beautifully written compass with the needle ever-pointing in the direction of hope.*" — Greg Yoder, grief counselor

"*So often we try to dance around our grief. This book offers the reader a safe place to do the healing work of "catch-up" mourning, opening the door to a life of freedom, authenticity and purpose.*"
— Kim Farris-Luke, bereavement coordinator

Are you depressed? Anxious? Angry? Do you have trouble with trust and intimacy? Do you feel a lack of meaning and purpose in your life? You may well be living in the shadow of the ghosts of grief.

When you suffer a loss of any kind—whether through abuse, divorce, job loss, the death of someone loved or other transitions, you naturally grieve inside. To heal your grief, you must express it. That is, you must mourn your grief. If you don't, you will carry your grief into your future, and it will undermine your happiness for the rest of your life.

This compassionate guide will help you learn to identify and mourn your carried grief so you can go on to live the joyful, whole life you deserve.

ISBN 978-1-879651-51-7 • 160 pages • softcover • $13.95

Also by Alan D. Wolfelt

Healing Your Grieving Heart

100 Practical Ideas

This flagship title in our 100 Ideas Series offers 100 practical ideas to help you practice self-compassion. Some of the ideas teach you the principles of grief and mourning. One of the most important ways to help yourself is to learn about the grief experience; the more you know, the less likely you will be to unknowingly perpetuate some of our society's most harmful myths about grief and healing.

The remainder offer practical, action-oriented tips for embracing your grief. Each idea is followed by a brief explanation of how and why the idea might help you. Each idea also suggests a carpe diem, which will help you seize the day by helping you move toward your healing today.

ISBN 978-1-879651-25-8 • 128 pages • softcover • $11.95

Also by Alan D. Wolfelt

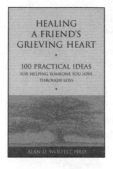

Healing A Friend's Grieving Heart

100 Practical Ideas for Helping Someone You Love Through Loss

When a friend suffers the loss of someone loved, you may not always know what to say. But you can do many helpful, loving things. Compassionate and eminently practical, *Healing A Friend's Grieving Heart* offers 100 practical ideas for friends, family members and caregivers who want to help. Some of the ideas teach the fundamentals of grief and mourning, while others offer practical, day-to-day ways to help. And each idea's carpe diem will help you seize the day by supporting your friend right now.

ISBN 978-1-879651-26-5 • 128 pages • softcover • $11.95